The Beauty of Black A to Z

Jacqueline Tyes

Illustrated by: Tyshaun Tyson

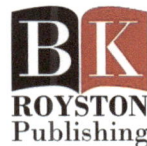

BK
ROYSTON
Publishing

BK Royston Publishing LLC

P. O. Box 4321

Jeffersonville, IN 47131

http://www.bkroystonpublishing.com

bkroystonpublishing@gmail.com

Cover Design & Illustrations: Tyshaun Tyson

Book Layout: BK Royston Publishing LLC

ISBN: 978-1-946111-69-2

Printed in the USA

Dedication

Dedicated to the memory of my beloved brother, Edwin Tyes Jr.

Acknowledgement

First and foremost, I'd like to thank God for with Him all things are possible.

I'd like to thank Tyshaun Tyson for his artistic contributions to making my dream a reality. You are truly amazing. I would like to thank my parents, Edwin and Marion Tyes for teaching me the importance of education, family, and following my dreams. I would also like to give a heartfelt thank you to my sisters, Jennifer, Theia, and Mariah for their inspiration, encouragement and unwavering support. I love you ladies unconditionally.

Finally, I would like to thank the love of my life, Zachary N. Smith II for always having an encouraging word and a listening ear. Your love and support is greatly appreciated.

Introduction

The Beauty of Black A to Z takes you on a journey of self-discovery, self-actualization, character building, and effective communication. It will explore ancestry, optimism and empower you to be bold and persistent in your daily life and in making your dreams a reality.

A is for AVID

Knowledge IS Freedom

Be an avid reader. Reading is essential in gaining the necessary knowledge to be a successful, productive, and gainfully employed citizen. Knowledge is the key to both mental and physical freedom.

B is for BELIEF

DREAMS

SUCCESS

Believe in yourself, in God, in family and in your community.
Do not depend on others to validate your position in this world.
You are who you say you are.
Belief in yourself will be the driving force for your success in life.

C is for COMMUNICATION

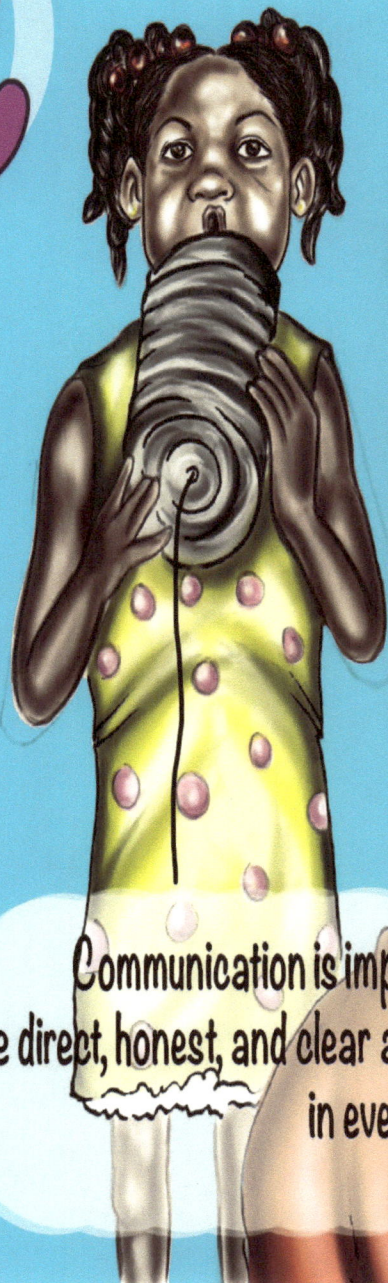

Communication is important to enhance your quality of life. Be direct, honest, and clear about the demands you have from people and in every aspect of your life.

D is for DETERMINATION

GOALS | ACTIONS

DETERMINATION

You must be determined to succeed. Be goal-oriented.
Be consistent in the steps that you take in achieving your goals.
Determination is one of the many keys to success.

E is for EDUCATION

Education is essential for advancement in life. It is important to continuously further your education so that you may build your marketability. Education breaks the chains of bondage. Education affords you the freedoms of endless possibilities.

F is for FAMILY

Family is needed as a support system as you encounter challenges in life. Family gives you direction and will hold you up when you feel like you are at the end of your rope.

G is for God

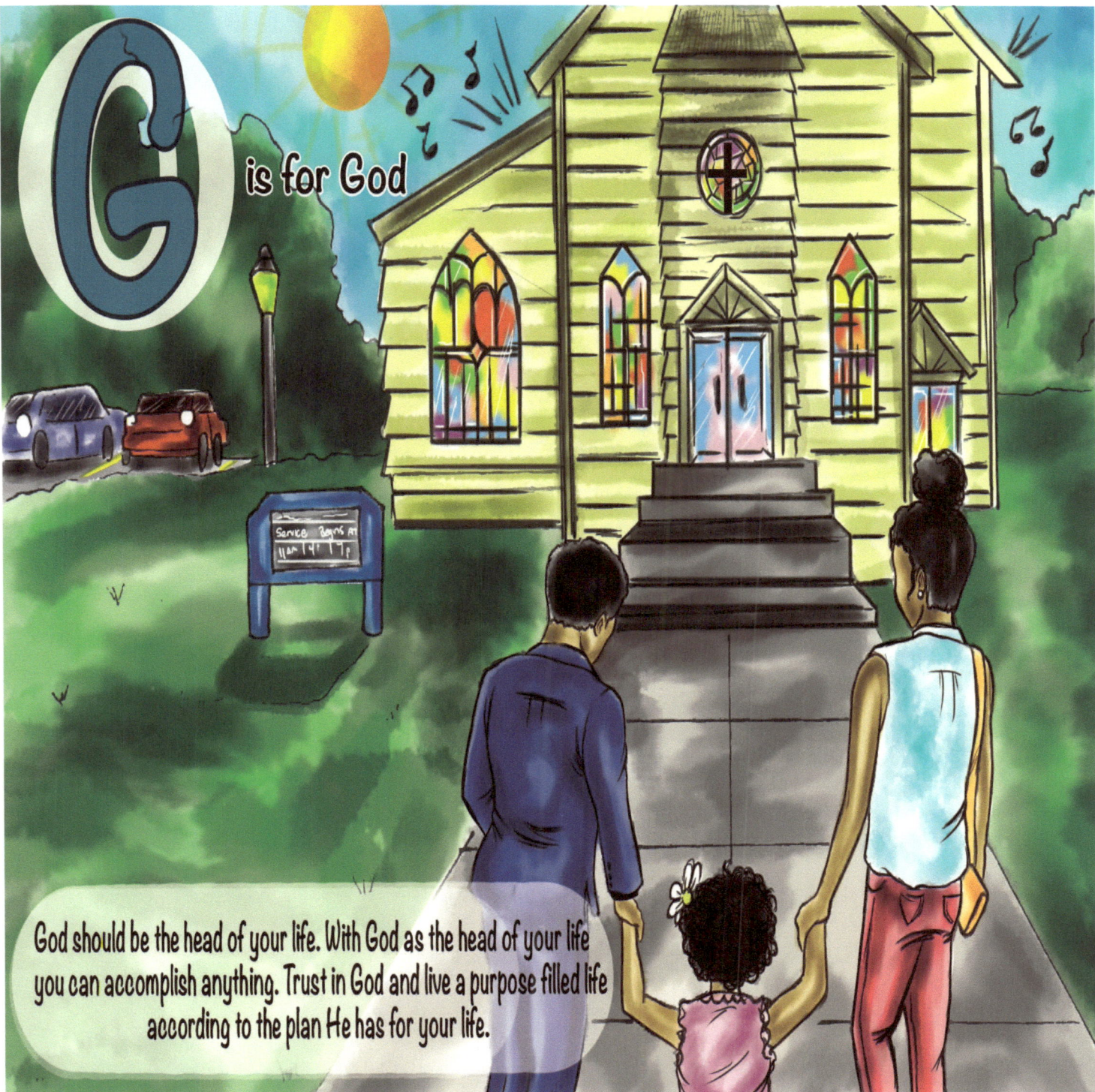

God should be the head of your life. With God as the head of your life you can accomplish anything. Trust in God and live a purpose filled life according to the plan He has for your life.

H

is for Honor

MAY GOD REST
HIS SOUL

Honor should be given to the great men and women who sacrificed, suffered and died to pave the way for the freedom that you enjoy today. Show honor by making great sound choices and by living a productive life.

is for INTEGRITY

WRONG WAY

INTEGRITY

Invest in yourself by walking with integrity in every aspect of your life.
Make great choices that will reflect positively on your character.
Take full responsibility for your actions and grow with each set back that you face.

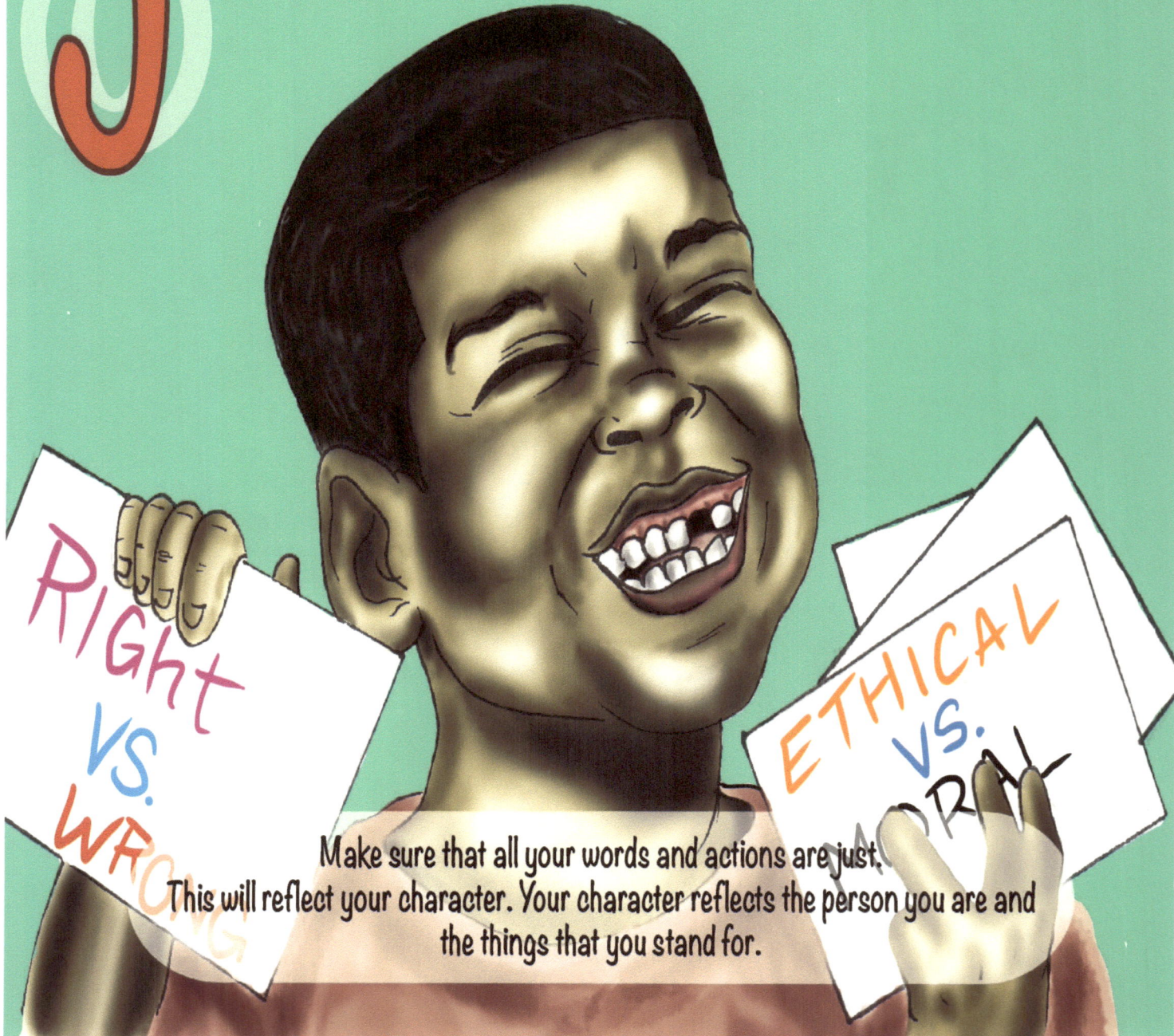

J is for JUST

RIGHT VS. WRONG

ETHICAL VS. MORAL

Make sure that all your words and actions are just. This will reflect your character. Your character reflects the person you are and the things that you stand for.

K

is for KWANZAA

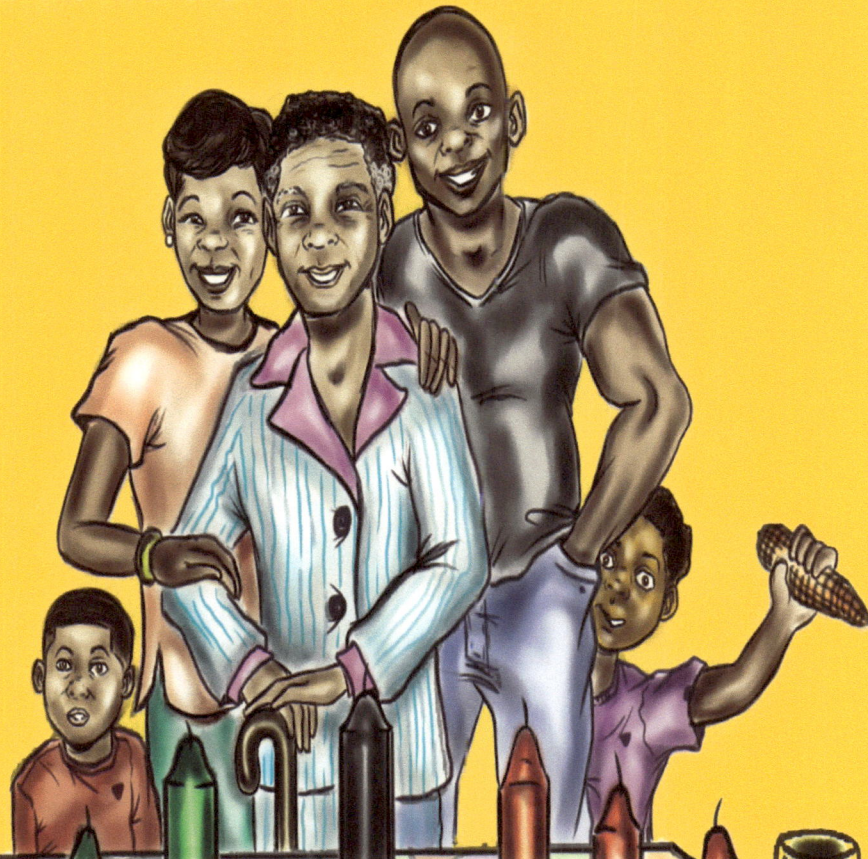

Kwanzaa is an African American Celebration of self-improvement, creativity, and family. Kwanzaa embodies unity in community. Kwanzaa is celebrated over the course of seven days with seven principles being at the core of each day.

L

is for LOVE

It is important to learn as many languages as possible. However, the most important language to learn is the language of love. Love can build bridges and tear down walls in your daily interactions with people. Therefore, you should communicate love in as many ways as you can to as many people as you can.

M

is for MUSIC

Music is a form of communication that dates back to the beginning of time. Music helps you to create and share memories that are important to your culture. Creating and sharing memories help to keep family traditions living so that they can be passed down from generation to generation. Music relaxes and comforts the soul.

N is for NATURAL

Be natural. Always accept yourself the way you are without making changes.
There is no need to make changes in efforts to be like anyone else.
You are perfect the way you are. Be exactly who you were
meant to be flaws and all. What may be perceived as a
flaw is actually a feature unique to you. You were born unique.
Everything about you makes you special. Your unique features make you who
you are. Be confident in who you are just the way you are.
Always strive to be different and stand out instead of blending in
with others. It is okay to stand out from everyone else.
Be a leader by paving a unique path in your journey in life.

O is for OPTIMISTIC

Choose to have a favorable view point of every situation.
Focusing on the positives in any given situation will
give you more joy and peace in your life.

P is for PRIDE

The things that you do and the places you go are a reflection of who you are. Therefore, you should always have pride in all that you do.

Q is for QUIT

Never quit! Always persevere. Perseverance builds character.

S is for STRENGTH

You are faced with challenges of the past and present. Strength helps you to endure these challenges.

T is for TREE

Your Family Tree represents your unique history. Knowing the richness of your history helps you to understand yourself. Knowing yourself helps you to make better choices in life. Make time to learn about your roots.

U

is for UNITY

You can always get more accomplished when working in unity with others. Unity promotes peace and growth. Working together will make life easier and better for all mankind.

V is for VOICE

Allow your voice to be heard.
Speak up for yourself and the things you believe in.
Your voice will help you obtain your victories.

W is for WISDOM

Wisdom is passed down by your ancestors.
Your ancestors paved the way so that your way would
be easier. It is important to take note of the wisdom being passed down
because it will help you to make better decisions for yourself.
As a result of paying close attention to your elders
you can learn from their mistakes which can make you even wiser.

X

is for eXtraordinary

You are extraordinary. In the pigment of your skin is a substance called Melanin. Melanin is a sign of strength.
It is a dominant, distinctive, and unique trait. Black is extraordinary.

Y is for YIELD

Put all of your energy into your creativity to reach your dreams.
Your hard work will yield great results.

Z is for ZEAL
You must have an eager interest in the pursuit of all things in order to achieve great things.

www.ingramcontent.com/pod-product-compliance
Lightning Source LLC
Chambersburg PA
CBHW060827270326
41931CB00002B/92